ALBERT'S INT!
ADVENT...

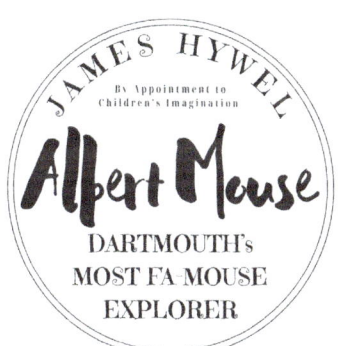

First published by Oink Books 2023
Copyright © 2023 by James Hywel

All rights reserved. No part of this publication may be reproduced, stored or transmitted in any form or by any means, electronic, mechanical, photocopying, recording, scanning, or otherwise without written permission from the publisher. It is illegal to copy this book, post it to a website, or distribute it by any other means without permission.

James Hywel asserts the moral right to be identified as the author of this work.

James Hywel has no responsibility for the persistence or accuracy of URLs for external or third-party Internet Websites referred to in this publication and does not guarantee that any content on such Websites is, or will remain, accurate or appropriate.

Designations used by companies to distinguish their products are often claimed as trademarks. All brand names and product names used in this book and on its cover are trade names, service marks, trademarks and registered trademarks of their respective owners. The publishers and the book are not associated with any product or vendor mentioned in this book. None of the companies referenced within the book has endorsed the book.

Although the publisher and the author have made every effort to ensure that the information in this book was correct at press time, the publisher and the author assume no responsibility for errors, including grammar and spelling mistakes. They will endeavour to rectify these in future editions.

Albert's Intriguing Salcombe Adventure

The Adventures of Albert Mouse
Book Nine

Created by
The pupils of Salcombe Church of England
Primary School in Salcombe.

&

James Hywel

OINK
BOOKS

Albert Books

The mouse who wanted to see the world

Albert and the smuggler Mickey Mustard

Albert takes to the sky

Albert and the runaway train

Albert buys a boat

Albert learns to swim

Albert's Christmas Adventure

Albert and the Mayor of Dartmouth

Albert's Intriguing Salcombe Adventure

Written for

Morgan & Josie

and

Mr Spike

This story was created by the pupils of **Salcombe Church of England Primary School**.
They created the title, wrote the initial story and provided the illustrations.

The *Albert Mouse Book for Schools Project* gives schools like Salcombe Church of England Primary School the unique opportunity to create their very own Albert Mouse story.

Chapter 1

Albert was sitting on the carpet looking at his atlas. The little mouse seemed very thoughtful.

His mother glanced at her son out of the corner of her eye. She always worried when he had his atlas open as it usually meant he was planning another adventure.

"Mum?" asked the little mouse eventually.

"Yes, Albert," replied his mother not looking up from her knitting.

"I think I might go to Salcombe," he said.

"Salcombe!?" replied his mother sounding surprised.

She had half expected him to say the word India, Africa, or even Australia and was very relieved it was only Salcombe.

"Yes, I've checked the map and it's only this far from Dartmouth," he said, holding up his two hands to indicate the distance on the map.

"And how do you plan to get there?" his mother asked.

"I don't know really. I suppose I could go by sea in my boat. There are some very interesting places I'd like to visit along the way," said the little mouse.

"Interesting, how?" asked Mrs Mouse.

"Well, I'd like to stop at Deadman's Cove," said Albert.

"I don't like the sound of that. It doesn't sound very safe," said his mother.

"Mum, it was probably given that name by pirates who had buried their treasure there and thought calling it Deadman's Cove would frighten away treasure hunters," said Albert.

The little mouse looked at his mother and could see that she wasn't happy about his first suggestion of a stopping point so he consulted the map again.

"Here's another place called Forest Cove."

"That sounds much more peaceful," said his mother. "Any others?"

Albert followed the shoreline with his finger but couldn't find any other coves.

"No, just lots of beaches," he sighed.

"Maybe going by boat is not such a good idea, Albert," said his mother.

"But, Mum, I've not been exploring with my boat since I bought it. And, anyway, I did learn to swim," he replied.

Mrs Mouse went back to her knitting and Albert continued to study his map.

Chapter 2

After Albert had finished studying his atlas, he decided to go and sit on the garden bench to enjoy the sunshine.

The little mouse stretched himself out and placed his hands behind his head. He closed his eyes and as he felt the sun warming his fur he started to imagine what it would be like to be a pirate and hiding chests full of treasure at Deadman's Cove.

Soon, Albert was asleep.

Dorothy, who had been watching her brother through the lounge window, fetched her sister. They both crept outside and sat on the doorstep watching their brother.

"Is he asleep?" whispered Millie.

"I think so. Listen, you can hear him snoring," giggled Dorothy.

After several minutes, the two girls tip-toed across the grass and stood in front of Albert. Dorothy picked up a tiny twig and was just about to tickle Albert's nose when her brother began to move his legs. First, it was a slight twitching, then more frantically.

"He's dreaming!" whispered Millie.

Albert was indeed dreaming. Dreaming he had just buried a large wooden treasure chest full of gold on the sandy beach at Deadman's Cove.

"The treasure should be safe here. Now let's get back to the ship," said Albert in his sleep.

Millie giggled.

"Shhh!" whispered Dorothy.

In his dream, Albert and his crew had just made it back to their ship when another pirate vessel came into the bay.

"Oh no, it's Captain Morgan and his pirate crew!" said the little mouse stretching out his arm and almost hitting Dorothy in the nose. "Load the canons and prepare to board! Fire!"

Albert's little legs began to move faster and faster as if he was running.

Soon his sisters were laughing so much that they woke Albert up.

He opened his eyes and looked around. At first, he didn't know where he was, but then he saw his two sisters laughing.

"What's so funny?" he asked sitting up.

"Prepare to board! Load the canons! Here comes Captain Albert, the silliest pirate to ever sail the seven seas!" laughed Dorothy.

Just then they heard the voice of their mother.

"I hope you're not annoying your brother," asked Mrs Mouse.

"Albert was dreaming about pirates," said Millie.

"I was not!" said Albert jumping off the bench and walking back to the house.

"Was so," laughed Dorothy.

"That's quite enough," said her mother.

Chapter 3

Mrs Mouse found her son sitting at the kitchen table with his head in his hands.

"Albert, I know your sisters annoy you but they only do it because you get cross," said his mother.

"They think I'm silly," said Albert. "They called me Captain Albert, the silliest pirate to ever sail the seas!"

"Yes, I heard them, but they are just saying that because deep down inside they want to be like you," said his mother.

"Really?" asked Albert, looking up at his mother.

"Yes, and I'm sure there are a lot of other children out there who think just the same. You know everyone likes you."

"Well, I'm going to show my sisters that I am not silly. In fact, I've made my mind up, I'm going to sail to Salcombe in my boat," said the little mouse.

Mrs Mouse looked at her son and sighed.

"Ok, but I don't want you going on your own," she said.

"I wasn't going to go on my own. I'll take Big Tony with me," he said.

"I was hoping for a more responsible adult," said his mother.

"Big Tony is very responsible. Remember how he delivered the flowers and fruit when I was Mayor?" replied Albert.

"Ok, maybe responsible wasn't the right word," said Mrs Mouse. "Possibly someone who is more knowledgeable of the sea," said Mrs Mouse.

"Mum, Big Tony IS knowledgeable about the sea," said Albert.

"Is he really?" asked Mrs Mouse, as she put the kettle on.

"Yes, he is. He might not have been to the Naval College but he is a seagull after all, and he wouldn't have the word sea in his name if he didn't know anything about it," said the little mouse.

"I'm not sure that really qualifies him to go to sea with you. Isn't there anyone else you can take with you?"

Albert thought for a moment and scratched his head. He tried to think of anyone he knew who might be more qualified than Big Tony to sail to Salcombe.

"I could always ask Mr Britton" suggested Albert.

"The Harbour Master? No, I think he will be far too busy to take time off work," said his mother as she placed a cup of tea and a slice of cake on the table next to her son.

"That's true," sighed Albert.

The little mouse picked up the cake and took a small bite.

"I've got it!" he said suddenly. "Of course! Why didn't I think of him before?"

"Who?"

"Reg, of course!" said Albert.

Mrs Mouse looked at her son with a confused look on her face.

"You know Reg, the rat with the wooden leg. He's spent years at sea with pirates. He probably knows these waters like the back of his hand," said Albert, feeling pleased with himself.

"Reg? With the wooden leg? I think I would feel safer if you went with Big Tony," said his mother.

Chapter 4

After Albert had finished his tea and cake he jumped off his chair.

"Well, I'd better go and have a chat with Reg," he said, putting on his flat cap. "I'll be back later."

Albert marched down to the gate, ignoring the comments from his sisters who were both now sitting on the wooden bench.

The little mouse cycled along Higher Street and turned right onto Smith Street, waving at people as they recognised him.

Eventually, Albert saw his friend Reg, sitting on a doorstep.

"Hi Albert, where are you off to?" asked the rat with the wooden leg.

"Nowhere. It's actually you I'm looking for. I need to talk to you about something," said the little mouse.

"Well, sit yourself down," said the rat, patting the stone step. "Now, what can I do for you?"

"You know I have a boat?" began Albert.

"Aye, a fine vessel if you don't mind me saying so. I've been down to the harbour to look at it a few times," said Reg.

"Thanks! The thing is I'm planning a trip out in it."

"A sea voyage!' said the rat. "How far are you going? West Indies, South America, Australia?"

"Erm, no, Salcombe," said the little mouse, feeling slightly embarrassed.

"Watch the bar is my advice," said Reg.

"Oh, I'm not old enough to drink yet," said Albert.

"The sand bar!" laughed Reg. "It's taken many a ship over the years, so it has."

"Oh, the sand bar, yes, well, of course I knew about that," said Albert nodding his head as if he knew what the rat was talking about.

The rat looked at his friend and could see that Albert didn't have a clue what he was talking about.

"Albert, you'd better come inside," he said and the little mouse followed Reg into the house.

The rat opened one of the cupboards and took out a map and unrolled it on the floor.

"We be here," he said, pointing to Dartmouth.

Albert nodded.

"This be Salcombe," said Reg, pointing to another inlet of sea similar to Dartmouth.

Albert nodded again.

"Now, there's nothing really to worry about until you get here," said Reg, pointing to a small island at the entrance to Salcombe.

The little mouse bent down and looked at the collection of rocks on the map.

"As you approach, make sure you stay to port and keep well clear of the rocks."

"Port?" asked Albert.

"Port is left and starboard is right. The front of the boat is called the bow and the back is the stern.

"I hope I will remember that," said Albert.

"Just remember 'the port left in the glass'. That's how us sailors remember it," said Reg.

Albert spent several hours listening to Reg talk about sailing and nautical terms before it was time for him to go home.

Chapter 5

When the little mouse reached his home he squeezed under the garden gate and walked up the path to the front door.

"Albert's back!" shouted Millie, who was looking out of the window.

Albert wiped his feet on the doormat, took off his hat and went into the lounge.

"You were a long time, how did you get on?" asked his mother.

"Fine. Reg knows so much about sailing and boats. He even gave me this sea chart for the trip," said the little mouse taking the rolled-up map out of his pocket.

"Is that a treasure map?" asked Millie.

"No, it's a navigation map," said Albert.

"So, has Reg agreed to go with you?" asked his mother.

"No, he said he is too old to be going to sea, but he's explained everything to me and says I'll be fine."

Mrs Mouse raised her eyebrows and looked at Albert, but before she could say anything Millie asked where Albert was planning to go.

"Salcombe," replied Albert as he unrolled the chart and began to explain his route.

"We are here and that is Salcombe," he said pointing to the various parts on the map.

"It looks an awfully long way," said Dorothy.

"It is but Reg has done the trip many times and said I can easily do it in my boat. Anyway, everything is fine until you enter the estuary to Salcombe," said her brother.

"Why, what happens then?" asked Mrs Mouse looking concerned.

Albert pointed to the small island that Reg had shown him.

"This is a rocky island that has wrecked many a ship. I'll be fine because to stay safe you just have to make sure you keep the island on your starboard side," smiled Albert. "That's what us sailors call the right side. Otherwise, you will end up on the sandbar."

"What's the left side called?" asked Millie.

"Port. The front of the boat is called the bow and the back is called the stern," said Albert feeling very knowledgeable.

His mother watched as her two daughters listened to Albert talk about his trip and she felt very proud of him.

"When are you going on this trip?" asked Millie.

"I'll probably leave in the morning," said Albert.

"Mum, can I go with Albert?" asked Millie.

"No, I think it's best you stay at home with me. Wouldn't you agree, Albert?"

"Yes, Mum's right. It's only a trip for experienced sailors like me and Big Tony," said her brother.

Millie looked very disappointed.

"Don't worry, I'll bring you a souvenir back from Salcombe," said Albert and then rolled up his map.

"Well, I'd better go and get my things ready for tomorrow," he said and went upstairs to his bedroom.

Chapter 6

In his bedroom, the little mouse went to the cupboard and lifted out his rucksack. He then placed it on his bed and scratched his head.

"Now, what else does a sailor need?" he asked himself but before he could think on the matter any further there was a familiar tap at the window.

"Oh, hello Big Tony, I was just going to call for you."

The gull looked at the rucksack and then at his friend.

"Where are you going?" he asked.

"We," said Albert with a broad grin. "Where are WE going."

"Oh, excellent. Another adventure! No, don't tell me, let me guess," said the gull as he hopped onto the window sill.

The gull thought for several moments but couldn't think of anywhere.

"Salcombe!" said the little mouse excitedly.

"Salcombe? Really?" replied Big Tony, sounding a little disappointed. "I thought you said it was an adventure."

"But it will be an adventure," said Albert. "Because we are going to go there in my boat!"

"Oh, wow, what in the sea, like real sailors?" said the gull smiling.

The little mouse nodded.

"When do we leave?" asked Big Tony.

"In the morning, about seven o'clock. I'm just packing now."

"Hang on, Albert, does your mother know about this?" asked the gull looking at his little friend.

"Of course she does. Did you think I would go on a sea adventure without telling her?" said the little mouse.

"Ok, I'm just checking," said the gull. "Well, I'll see you later then."

The gull then launched himself out of the window and was gone.

Alone again, Albert went back to his packing.

He placed a change of clothes neatly in the rucksack.

"Compass!" he said suddenly and opened the drawer of his bedside cupboard and picked up the compass that Father Christmas had given him.

Just then there was a knock at his bedroom door.

"It's just me," said his mother as she came into the room. "How is the packing going?"

"Good. I'm taking a change of clothes and my compass so I can navigate," said her son.

"Do you want me to make you a packed lunch?" asked his mother.

"No, we will be fine, thanks. Big Tony and I can get lunch in Salcombe," said Albert.

"I'd feel happier if you at least had a sandwich to take with you," said his mother.

Mrs Mouse left Albert packing his bag and went downstairs.

Chapter 7

Later that evening Albert unrolled his map and studied his route several times. Soon it was time for bed, so the little mouse said goodnight to his mother and went up to bed.

When Albert woke up it was still dark. He climbed out of bed, put his clothes on and as quietly as possible he went to the bathroom to clean his teeth.

When he got back to his bedroom he saw Big Tony sitting on the window ledge.

"I saw your light was on, so I knew you were awake," said the gull.

"I couldn't sleep," replied the little mouse. "I think I am too excited!"

"Me too!" said Big Tony. "Oh, I've brought my telescope, I thought we might need it."

"Good thinking," said Albert placing it in his rucksack.

The two friends then crept downstairs and went into the kitchen.

"Would you like some breakfast?" asked Albert.

"No, thanks, I've just eaten half a pasty left over from yesterday.

Albert made himself a bowl of cereal and sat down at the table.

"You're up very early," said his mother as she came into the kitchen.

"Neither of us could sleep. I think we are both too excited," said the little mouse.

His mother went to the fridge, took out a small sandwich box and gave it to Albert.

"I know you said you would be fine but I've made you both some lunch just in case you get hungry on the journey."

"Thanks, Mum," said Albert, hugging his mother.

The little mouse then looked at Big Tony.

"Well, I suppose we had better get going," he said putting the sandwiches in his rucksack.

"Now, you have got everything, haven't you?" asked his mother.

The little mouse nodded.

"Please be careful, both of you," she said.

"Don't worry, Mrs Mouse, I'll make sure I look after him," said Big Tony.

"And I'll look after him," added Albert with a smile.

The two friends walked to the front door. They both hugged Mrs Mouse.

"Bye, Mum, I love you," said Albert as he and the gull walked down to the gate.

"I love you too," said his mother.

Chapter 8

Quite a crowd had gathered on the quayside to wish the two friends well on their adventure.

The Harbour Master was there, and so were Mrs Saunders and Reg the rat. Even the Mayor was waiting to say goodbye.

"Albert, I have a special letter I would like you to deliver to the Mayor of Salcombe on my behalf," said Mr Wells, as he handed the little mouse an envelope with a red seal on the back.

"Of course," said Albert, placing the envelope in his rucksack.

Albert then turned to the crowd.

"Thank you everyone for getting up so early to say goodbye to me and Big Tony. We know that this journey is full of danger but as experienced explorers, we follow in the footsteps of the passengers of the Mayflower. Like them, we will carry the memories of home in our hearts as we battle the sea. We hope to return soon to Dartmouth, the greatest town in the world."

Everyone applauded.

"Three cheers for Albert and Big Tony! Hip hip hooray!" they shouted.

Albert and Big Tony walked down the pontoon and climbed into their boat.

"Ready?" asked Albert looking at his friend.

"Ready!" said the gull.

The two friends cast off the ropes and slowly the small boat pulled away from the mooring. It then made its way into the harbour, heading towards the small gap of open water and the sea beyond.

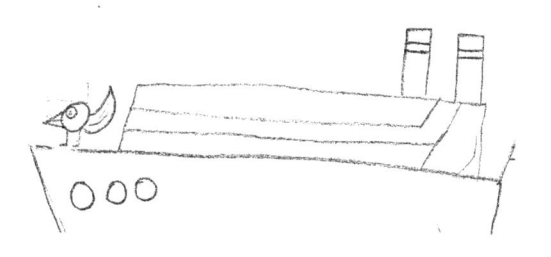

Back at No.10 Higher Street, Mrs Mouse could hear the cheering crowds.

Dorothy and Millie had heard the noise and came downstairs to stand on the doorstep with their mother.

"Are they cheering for Albert?" asked Millie.

"Yes, it would appear so. I do hope he's going to be ok," said her mother sounding very worried.

"Please don't worry, Albert will be fine," said Dorothy. "Anyway, Big Tony won't let anything happen to him."

"I hope you're right," sighed her mother. "I hope you're right."

Chapter 9

The small boat was making good progress and soon it passed Dartmouth Castle.

"Isn't this amazing!?" said Big Tony, who was standing at the front of the boat.

"It certainly is," agreed the little mouse. "This is already the best adventure ever. Look, you can see the canons sticking out of those windows up there. Can you imagine being a pirate ship with those firing at you?"

Albert quickly looked at the chart that Reg had given him.

"That's Castle Cove and the next one coming up is Sugary Cove," shouted Albert, pointing to a small beach near the castle.

The little mouse then looked ahead and saw that the sea just went on and on forever.

"I guess that is the whole world out there," he thought to himself and then looked down at his map again.

"Deadman's Cove coming up on the starboard side!" announced the little mouse.

Big Tony took the telescope out of Albert's rucksack and held it up to his eye.

"I can't see any dead men," he said.

"Phew! That's a relief," said Albert. "My compass says we are now heading in a south-westerly direction."

The two friends continued along the coastline, passing Compass Cove, Willow Cove and Shiglehill Cove.

"Watch the rocks!" shouted Big Tony, pointing to some large rocks a little way ahead of them.

"Thanks, Big Tony," said Albert as he steered around them. "That's Inner Combe Rocks."

Soon a long, curved stretch of sand came into view.

"Wow, Albert, look at that," said the gull.

Albert looked down at his chart.

"That must be Blackpool Sands," he said.

On and on the two friends went until another, even longer stretch of sand came into view.

"What's that one called asked Big Tony pointing.

"I think that's Slapton Sands," replied Albert, looking at his map.

On and on they went, until they passed Start Point Lighthouse.

"Are we nearly there yet?" asked Big Tony.

The little mouse looked down at his map.

"We've passed the halfway point so soon there should be an inlet that looks very similar to Dartmouth," said Albert.

Big Tony held his telescope up.

"I can't see anything yet," he said as the little boat bobbed up and down in the waves.

Chapter 10

Suddenly Big Tony became very excited.

"Is that it, over there, Albert?!" he said pointing towards what looked like an opening in the coastline.

The little mouse quickly looked at his sea chart.

"Yes, that's it. Well spotted!"

Albert slowly turned the boat to starboard and entered the estuary. He knew that this was going to be the most dangerous part of the whole journey. As he remembered what Reg had told him about the 'bar' his little heart began to race.

"Keep your eyes open for a rocky island," shouted the little mouse.

The gull looked through his telescope.

"Albert, it's straight ahead of us!" replied Big Tony.

Albert slowed the engine down and quickly turned the boat hard to port.

"That's it Albert, good work," shouted the gull as their little boat managed to avoid the island and the sand bar.

"Phew," he thought to himself as he looked at the jagged rocks that would have smashed his boat to pieces. The little mouse felt pleased with himself that he had remembered what Reg had told him.

As they went further up the estuary the water became calmer. Albert began to relax a little and he felt the warm breeze on his back.

"Oooh, can you smell that?" asked Big Tony. "We must be getting close to the harbour."

Albert sniffed the air and instantly recognised the smell of freshly baked pasties. Soon a series of wooden pontoons came into view.

"We'll tie up over there," said the little mouse pointing to one of the jetties with a space that was just big enough for Albert's boat.

As Big Tony tied the boat to the jetty, Albert rolled up his chart and placed it in his rucksack. He then put his compass in his pocket.

The two friends then walked along the wooden jetty towards the buildings that were on the quayside.

"It looks a bit like Dartmouth," said Albert looking around. "It even smells the same."

"So, what are going to do first?" asked the gull.

Albert suddenly remembered the letter that Mr Wells had given him for the Mayor of Salcombe.

"I'd better drop the letter off first," he said.

"Ok, you do that while I look for my relatives. They are bound to know the best place to get some pasties," said Big Tony.

Chapter 11

Albert was just arranging when and where to meet Big Tony after he had dropped off the letter, when, out of nowhere, wailing sirens pierced the little mouse's ears.

"What was that!?" he exclaimed, looking around.

Seconds later men and women dressed in heavy waterproof suits dashed out of a building and ran towards where the two friends were standing.

"Are we in trouble?" asked Big Tony looking at Albert.

"I hope not," said the little mouse looking very worried.

The men and women ran along the jetty, past where the friends were standing and climbed onboard a large orange and blue boat.

"They are the lifeboat crew!" smiled Albert, as he watched the crew quickly undock the boat and start the engines. The large boat then sped away from the jetty, heading towards the open sea.

"Wow!" said Albert. "I'd love to have a go on that boat. Did you see how fast it went?"

Big Tony seemed more interested in finding some of his relatives, so Albert said goodbye to him and headed towards the quayside.

The little mouse walked along the narrow street where the Life Boat people had come from and, as he turned into Union Street, he saw the Lifeboat Shop.

"Hello, I wonder if you can help me?" he said, as he opened the shop door. "My name is Albert Mouse and I'm looking for the Mayor's office."

"Ah, you'll need the Council Offices then. They are on Cliff Road. Just go to the end of the street here and turn left onto Fore Street and just keep going straight. Fore Street runs into Cliff Road. When you see the War Memorial on your left-hand side, the Town Council is on the right-hand side. It's a big building, you really can't miss it," said the helpful man.

"Thank you very much," said Albert and with that he went back out into the street and followed the directions the man had given him.

Luckily for Albert, the streets were quiet. The traffic seemed to all be going the same way, which the little mouse was very glad about.

Albert walked quite a way and was just beginning to think he'd taken a wrong turn when he suddenly saw the War Memorial and then the large building on the right.

Chapter 12

The little mouse climbed up the steep steps that lead up from the street and eventually reached the door of the Council Offices.

"Hello, I'd like to see the Mayor, please," he said to the person at the reception desk.

"Do you have an appointment?" asked the lady.

"Erm, no, not really," said Albert.

"Well, if you don't have an appointment you can't see her," replied the lady quite firmly.

Albert opened his rucksack and took out the letter.

"I've come all the way from Dartmouth to deliver this letter," he said. The lady took the envelope and looked at it.

"Who gave you this?" she asked, noticing the red wax seal on the back of the envelope.

"Mr Wells, he's the Mayor of Dartmouth and he asked me to deliver it for him."

The lady looked over her spectacles at the little mouse.

"And who are you?" she asked.

"My name is Albert Mouse," he said proudly.

"Oh goodness, why didn't you say so in the first place," she said and picked up the phone.

"Hello, I have Albert Mouse in reception to see you. Yes, that Albert Mouse, from Dartmouth. He has a letter for you."

The lady put the phone down and almost immediately a door opened and the Mayor came into the reception area.

"Albert, what a pleasure to meet you! I've heard so much about you," she said, shaking his hand. "Would you like a cup of hot chocolate and some biscuits?"

"No, thank you. I just came to give you this," he said handing over the letter. "I'm only here for the day and need to get back to Dartmouth before dark otherwise my mother will worry."

"I understand. So, what are your plans for the rest of the day?" asked the Mayor.

"We are not sure. This is our first time in Salcombe," replied the little mouse.

"We?" asked the Mayor looking around.

"I'm here with my friend Big Tony. He's just looking for a good pasty shop."

"Oh, well, if it's a good pasty you want, let me recommend the Bake House. Tell Ben I sent you. After that, you should visit Salcombe Dairy. They make the best ice cream in the world," added the Mayor.

"Thanks! I do like ice cream," said Albert. "Well, I'd better go and find Big Tony."

"Oh, I almost forgot," said the Mayor just before she turned to go back to her office. "If you have time you should visit North Sands, it's a lovely beach and just a few minutes from here at the end of Cliff Road."

"Thank you!" said Albert and waved goodbye.

Chapter 13

Once outside, Albert sat on the grass outside the Council Offices for several minutes and looked across the estuary. He watched the small boats going back and forth and wondered if any of them were going to Dartmouth.

"It is very beautiful here," he said to himself as he watched the sea glittering like diamonds in the sunlight. "I wish my Mum was here to see it."

The little mouse then remembered what the Mayor had said about North Sands. Since he wasn't yet hungry, Albert decided to take a look and set off along Cliff Road.

As he walked he lifted his cap and politely said hello to everyone he met. Eventually, he came around a corner and wasn't prepared for the sight that greeted him. There, below the road, was the most loveliest of beaches. He could see families sitting on the sand, and children playing in the shallow water.

"Oh, wow!" said Albert.

The little mouse rushed down the road and onto the sand. Finding a quiet spot,

Albert took off his rucksack and sat down on the warm sand. He rested back against his rucksack and put his hands behind his head to watch the waves gently crashing onto the beach.

Just then a small dog that had been running in and out of the water came over and sniffed the little mouse.

"Don't worry, he's very friendly!" said a little girl, picking up the small dog. "His name is Spaghetti and mine's Alice. What's your name?"

"Hello, my name is Albert," he replied. "I'm very pleased to meet you, Alice."

"Do you live here in Salcombe? It's just I haven't seen you before."

"No, I live in Dartmouth. I'm just here for the day with my friend Big Tony," said Albert.

"I've never been to Dartmouth, is it nice?" asked Alice.

"Dartmouth is the best place in the whole world," smiled the little mouse.

The little girl didn't seem too impressed by Albert's description of Dartmouth.

"Me and Spaghetti have been swimming. Can you swim?" she asked, looking at the little mouse.

"I certainly can," said Albert. "But I've never swum in the sea before though, just a swimming pool."

"It's very much the same," said Alice. "I'm going to go back in with Spaghetti. You can come with us if you like."

"Yes, ok, but will my things be safe if I leave them here?" asked Albert.

"Of course, don't worry," said Alice and she ran off into the water with her dog.

Albert quickly took off his cap, jacket and shirt, and placed them neatly in his rucksack. He then rolled up his trouser legs as high as they could go and walked across the sand.

Chapter 14

As he reached the water's edge the little mouse hesitated and then ran back away from the approaching water.

"Don't be scared, Albert," shouted Alice as she splashed about in the waves.

The little mouse smiled at his new friend and let the next wave wash over his feet.

"That is freezing!" he said to himself as he shivered.

"Once you're in it's fine," shouted the little girl in encouragement.

Albert counted to three and then ran into the sea.

Despite what Alice had said, the water was still freezing and Albert's hands, feet and tail were soon numb with the cold. Albert jumped up as each wave approached to keep his head above the water.

"It will be warmer if you swim, instead of just standing there," shouted Alice.

Anything was worth a try so the little mouse lent forward and began to swim.

"There, see! Isn't that better?" asked the little girl.

Frankly, it wasn't. Even though Albert was paddling as fast as he could with both his legs and arms he didn't seem to be going anywhere.

"This is far harder than in a swimming pool," thought Albert and was soon out of breath, so he turned around and began swimming back to the beach.

Suddenly the little mouse felt something grab the end of his tail.

"Ouch!" he exclaimed, and then tried to pull his tail free but whatever the creature was, it just wouldn't let go.

Soon Albert felt himself being dragged backwards, away from the beach and into deeper water.

He then remembered how Daisy had taught him how to put his head into the bucket of water. He took several deep breaths and then plunged his head down into the water to try and see what was holding his tail.

Instantly the salty water stung his eyes but he did manage to stay underwater just long enough to see that the creature that was holding the end of his tail was actually a very large crab.

Albert lifted his head out of the water and gasped for breath. He then looked around and saw he was now even further from the shore than before.

The little mouse knew that if he didn't do something quickly the crab might start to eat him. So, he took a few more deep breaths and then dived down and wrestled his tail out of the crab's claw.

Albert swam back to the surface quickly and tucked his tail into his pocket just in case the crab came back.

He then rubbed his eyes and looked around but the beach was so far away that he couldn't even see the people and he certainly couldn't see Alice. He began to swim as hard as he could, but no matter how fast he paddled with his arms and legs the beach just kept getting further and further away.

Soon the little mouse was exhausted and very frightened.

He looked up at the blue sky hoping that he would see Big Tony because he knew he would rescue him, but his friend was nowhere to be seen.

Chapter 15

Back at the shore, Alice ran to her parents.

"I think Albert's been carried out to sea," she said, crying.

"Who is Albert?" asked her mother.

"He's my new friend. I met him this morning. I think the current has washed him away and it's all my fault," she said, sobbing.

"There, there. Don't worry, I'll call the lifeboat," said her mother, taking her phone out of her pocket.

After a few rings, a man answered the phone at the RNLI station.

"Yes, hello. We are at North Sands and my daughter was swimming with her friend and we think he has been caught in a current and washed out to sea," she said.

"Ok, don't panic. We will have a crew there right away. In the meantime, what is the boy's name?" said the man.

"Albert," said Alice's mother.

"And how old is Albert?" asked the RNLI man.

The lady looked at her daughter.

"They want to know how old Albert is," she said.

"Let me speak to them," said Alice, taking the phone from her mother. "Hello, My name is Alice. I'm really not sure how old Albert is."

"Ok, can you describe him to me?" asked the man on the end of the phone.

"Yes, I can do that. He has large round ears and a long tail."

"Hang on, you said large round ears and a tail. Is Albert your dog?' asked the man.

"No, my dog is called Spaghetti. Albert is a mouse," said Alice sounding impatient.

"A mouse?"

"Yes, he's wearing trousers, which he has rolled up because he didn't have his swimming costume with him," added Alice. "Oh, and he lives in Dartmouth, which he says is the best place in the whole world, which I doubt very much because everyone knows Salcombe is the best place in the whole world."

"Did you say he's from Dartmouth?" asked the man.

"Yes! You really don't seem to be listening. We are just wasting time while my friend could be, well, he could be anywhere by now," said Alice sounding very cross and very worried.

"Can you pass me back to your mother, please, Alice?"

"He wants to speak to you," sighed Alice.

Her mother took the phone.

"Hello? I'm awfully sorry, it seems my daughter was just wasting your valuable time making up stories about a mouse."

"No, she has done precisely the right thing. We know who Albert Mouse is and a lifeboat should be arriving any minute now to conduct a search of the area.

Please tell your daughter we will do everything we can to find Albert," interrupted the man.

Chapter 16

By now Albert didn't know where he was and was feeling very scared and alone. He began to wonder if he would ever see his family again and, as he bobbed up and down in the sea, he began to cry.

He was about to lose all hope when suddenly the little mouse heard the faint sound of an engine and he looked around.

"Hello, I'm over here!" he shouted and waved his arms as a large orange and blue boat came into view.

"A lifeboat," thought Albert. "I'm going to be saved!"

But instead of coming straight towards him, the lifeboat seemed to be turning away and going out to sea.

"NO! I'm over here!" he shouted again as loud as he could, but it was no use.

Tears filled Albert's eyes as he watched the lifeboat get smaller and smaller.

"I'm never going to be rescued," sobbed the little mouse.

Suddenly the lifeboat changed direction again. This time it seemed to be heading straight for where Albert was.

The little mouse raised his arms and began waving.

"Over here!" he shouted.

Just then a voice came over the loudspeaker system on the boat.

"Hello Albert, we can see you. Just stay calm and we will soon have you safely onboard," said the voice.

The large lifeboat came to a stop next to the little mouse and one of the crew lent over and scooped the little mouse up in his hand.

"There you are Albert, you're safe now. Let's get you nice and warm," said the lady as she wrapped the shivering mouse up in a small blanket.

One of the other crew picked up the radio and called the RNLI Station.

"Albert is safe. He is just being checked over and having a warm drink. We are heading back to base," said the man.

"I'm so sorry I've caused you so many problems," said Albert, still shivering.

"Please don't worry yourself. These things can easily happen, even to the most experienced swimmers like yourself," said the lady.

"I would have been ok if the crab hadn't grabbed my tail in its claw and dragged me into deeper water. Luckily I managed to escape," said Albert. "But as I tried to swim back to shore it just felt like I was being dragged back out to sea. At first, I thought it was the crab again."

"I think you must have been caught in a rip-tide. It's a very strong current," said the lady. "Anyway, you're safe now, that's the important thing."

Another member of the crew brought Albert a cup of hot chocolate.

"How is he doing?" he asked.

"He's fine. A little shaken and cold. It seems he was caught in a rip tide," replied the lady.

"And a large crab," said Albert, showing the man the bite marks on his tail.

The man examined the claw marks.

"You've had a very lucky escape! But I think you'll be ok now," he said.

Chapter 17

The large lifeboat turned and was heading back to the lifeboat station with Albert when suddenly the engines stopped.

"What's happened?" asked the little mouse sipping his hot chocolate.

"I'm not sure. You stay there and I'll go and check," said the lady.

A few minutes later she came back.

"It seems the boat's propeller is caught on a fishing line," she said.

"Oh no, this is all my fault," sighed the little mouse.

"No, it's not, Albert. Anyway, don't worry because we have called the lifeboat station and they are launching the D-

Class lifeboat to take you into Salcombe. It should be here in a few minutes."

It didn't take long for the smaller lifeboat to arrive and the crew soon had Albert transferred onto the smaller lifeboat.

"Hold on tight, Albert!" said the crewman. "It can get a bit bouncy on the waves."

Albert did as he was told because he certainly didn't want to fall into the sea again.

The crew of the D-Class waved goodbye to the larger lifeboat and rushed back to the lifeboat station where a small crowd of people had gathered.

"Please stand back," said one of the crew as they carried Albert ashore and headed towards the Lifeboat Station where the doctor was waiting.

The doctor examined Albert thoroughly and then said that the little mouse didn't need to go to the hospital, much to everyone's relief.

"Thank you so much for saving my life," said Albert, as he shook everyone's hand.

"That's what we are here for," said one of the crew.

"I'm very grateful you are. You are all very brave," said Albert.

Albert waved goodbye to everyone and went down the stairs, out onto Union Street.

"Albert, there you are! I've been so worried about you, wherever have you been?" asked Big Tony running up the road.

"It's a very long story but I'm fine now," said Albert.

The gull looked at his friend.

"Erm, where is your shirt?" he asked.

"Oh no, I left it on the beach at North Sands with my rucksack!" said Albert looking worried.

"I don't know, I leave you alone for five minutes and look what happens," laughed Big Tony. "You stay right here and I'll fly over to North Sands and collect your things.

"Oh, there is a little girl there who will probably be worried about me. Her name is Alice and she has a dog called Spaghetti. Can you just tell her I'm safe?" asked Albert.

"No problem, now try and stay out of trouble until I get back," said Big Tony.

"I'll be right there, sitting on that bench," said the little mouse pointing to a seat on the quayside.

With that, Big Tony flapped his wings and lifted himself into the air. After flying in a few circles the gull headed off in the direction of North Sands.

Chapter 18

While Albert waited for his friend to return he sat down on the bench and soaked up the warm sun.

"Gosh, I'm hungry," he thought to himself as the smell of freshly baked pasties filled the air.

The little mouse wondered if he had time to run and get a pasty, but then realised that his money was in his rucksack on the beach at North Sands.

Albert then remembered that the sea chart and his compass were in the rucksack.

"Oh no, I hope someone hasn't taken my bag, because we need those to get home," he said.

The little mouse decided to cross his fingers and toes and hope that Big Tony was able to find the rucksack.

Over at North Sands Big Tony was circling over the beach but he couldn't see Albert's rucksack anywhere.

Just then he spotted a little girl with a small dog sitting on the sand looking out to sea. The gull glided down and gently landed on the sand next to the little girl.

"Hello, are you Alice?"

"Yes, who are you?" she asked.

"My name is Big Tony."

"You're Albert's friend!" said Alice looking happier. "Is he ok?"

"Albert's fine. It looks like he had to be rescued by the Lifeboat, but apart from that he's fine," said the gull.

"You don't know how worried I was about him. One minute he was there and the next he was gone. I was worried that maybe he had been eaten by a large fish," said Alice.

"The thing is he left his rucksack on the beach and I can't seem to see it," said Big Tony.

"Don't worry. When I realised that Albert had been washed away by the sea I took his bag to my mum to make sure it was safe from the incoming tide. She's over there," replied Alice getting up.

"Mum, this is Big Tony. He's Albert's friend," said Alice to her mother.

"Is Albert ok?" asked Alice's mother.

"He's fine," said Big Tony. "Luckily the lifeboat picked him up and I've just come to pick up his bag."

"Yes, here it is," said Alice's mother.

The gull put the rucksack on his back and tightened the straps.

"Is Albert famous?" asked Alice.

"You could say that," smiled Big Tony, winking at Alice.

Big Tony said goodbye to Alice and her mother. He found an empty stretch of sand and after a few steps, the gull lifted himself into the air and flew back to the quayside where Albert was waiting.

Chapter 19

Back at the bench, Albert had closed his eyes to soak up the warmth of the sun. He didn't see Big Tony land next to him.

"Albert, are you asleep?" whispered the gull in the little mouse's ear.

Albert opened his eyes.

"Oh, you're back!" he exclaimed. "And you've found my rucksack!"

"Yes, when Alice realised you'd been washed away she gave your bag to her mother for safekeeping," said the gull, taking the rucksack off his back.

"Did you meet your relatives?" asked Albert as he quickly took his shirt out and got dressed.

"Yes, and I'll tell you what, they are a really noisy bunch. Talk about chat, I was glad to get away," said Big Tony.

"And have you had lunch?" asked Albert.

"No, not yet," replied Big Tony.

"Well, the Mayor of Salcombe has recommended the Bake House, so shall we go there? I heard they make delicious pasties."

"Now you're talking!" said the gull smiling broadly.

The two friends set off up Union Street.

"There it is," said Albert, pointing at the large grey shop that said 'The Bake House' above the door.

"Hello, my name is Albert and this is my friend Big Tony. The Mayor said we should ask for a man called Ben," said the little mouse as he went inside the shop.

"I'm Ben, I'm pleased to meet you. How can I help?" said the man behind the counter.

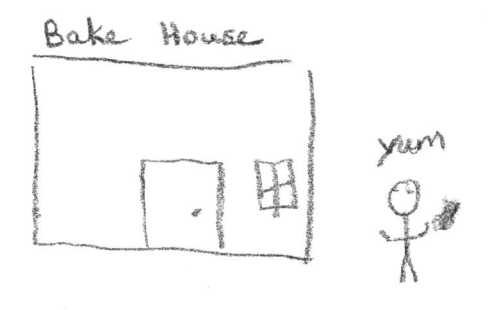

Albert looked at his friend.

"You're having a pastie, right?" he asked.

"Yes, please, and make it a large one," replied Big Tony.

"And I'd like a large sausage roll, please," said Albert.

"Good choice," said Ben as he put the items in a paper bag.

Albert paid and then said goodbye to Ben.

"He was a very nice man," said Big Tony when they got outside.

The two friends found another bench and sat down to eat their lunch.

"How's your pastie?" asked Albert.

"Really tasty," said the gull with his mouth full. "Yours?"

"Mmm, really good. I hadn't realised how hungry I was," said the little mouse.

As they ate their lunch they watched the people going about their business.

"Isn't it nice no one recognises us here?" said Albert. "In Dartmouth, we would be signing autographs and having people ask if they could have their photo taken with us. He we are just normal people and not celebrities."

"You know, I hadn't thought about that, but you're right," said Big Tony.

When they had finished their lunch they sat in the sun and leisurely watched the world go by.

Chapter 20

Soon Albert and Big Tony became bored watching people so they decided to explore Salcombe and set off along Fore Street.

"Oh, look, a sweet shop!" said Albert, looking in the window of Cranch's. "Wow, it says it's Devon's oldest sweet shop!"

They both bustled quickly inside the shop. Albert stood in amazement as he looked at all the jars of sweets that filled the shelves.

"You weren't expecting to see so many different sweets were you," said the man behind the counter.

"I certainly wasn't! My name is Albert by the way, and this is my friend, Big Tony," said the little mouse.

"Hello, my name is Peter," replied the man.

"Is this shop really the oldest sweet shop in Devon?" asked Big Tony.

"It certainly is. This shop has been here since 1869 and was opened by Mrs Cranch and her three daughters," said Peter.

"Are they your relatives?" asked Big Tony.

"No, the shop was sold to Mr Yeoman in 1970 and my father bought the shop from him in 1980," smiled Peter.

Peter glanced at the little mouse and could see him trying to count on his fingers.

"If you are trying to work out how long ago 1869 was it's one hundred and fifty-four years," said Peter.

Albert wondered if that was when the dinosaurs lived but he decided to check that when he got home. He would be able to borrow a book from Mrs Saunders at the bookshop.

"So, what can I get you both?" asked Peter.

The little mouse looked again at all the jars of sweets. He just couldn't make up his mind.

"How about I put a mixed selection of our most popular sweets in a bag for you?" suggested Peter.

"That sounds like an excellent idea," said Albert. "But could we have five bags? I need to give one each to my mother and my two sisters. Their names are Dorothy and Millie."

"Five bags it is then," said Peter picking up some lovely pink and white striped paper bags.

When Albert had paid for the sweets he and Big Tony said goodbye to Peter and went back out into the street.

"Where shall we go now?" asked Big Tony.

"I think we deserve some ice cream," said Albert and the two friends headed off in the direction of Island Street.

Chapter 21

As they turned into Island Street, Big Tony looked about.

"Are you sure this is the right street? It just looks like a lot of houses," the gull said.

The little mouse was beginning to think the same thing so he stopped some people coming towards them.

"Hello, is this the way to Salcombe Dairy?" Albert asked.

"The factory or the dairy?" replied the man.

"Erm, I'm not sure. We are looking for ice cream," replied Albert.

"Ice creams are at the end of the road on the left, but the factory is just ahead on the right. That's where they make the chocolate," said the man.

"Thank you," said Albert, lifting his cap slightly.

"Did you hear that, Albert? Chocolate!" smiled Big Tony.

"Mmm, we will have to stop there first," smiled the little mouse.

The two friends passed a large building which had lots of boats inside, then several other shops.

"Here it is!" said Albert, as he sniffed the air several times and recognised the delicious smell of chocolate.

The little mouse looked up at the large sign across the building.

"Salcombe Dairy Chocolate Factory. This is definitely the place," he said.

He pushed the door open and they stepped inside the building.

"Hello, my name is Rita. Would you like to look around the chocolate factory?" asked the lady.

"Yes, please," smiled Albert.

"Well, we opened our chocolate factory and shop in July 2022. Here you can experience the sights and sounds of our chocolate being made," said Rita.

"And the delicious smell," added Albert.

"It is good, isn't it?" smiled Rita. "Here we make all sorts of chocolate items including Easter eggs, Advent calendars, hot chocolate and hampers full of chocolate things."

"Mmm, hot chocolate is my favourite drink, but I also like milkshakes," said the little mouse.

"And have you tried The Bar, our famous yummy chocolate bar?"

The two friends shook their heads.

"It's very tasty and we make twenty different flavours," said Rita.

"Is it named after the bar in the estuary?" asked Albert.

"Of course!" smiled Rita.

"Big Tony and I sailed passed that as we came into the harbour," said Albert.

"So, how is the chocolate made?" asked Big Tony.

"Well, if you follow me I'll show you," said the lady.

Chapter 22

Rita lead the two visitors over to a counter where there were several large jars of beans.

"It all starts here with the cocoa beans which are then ground into chocolate. Do you know where the beans come from?" Rita asked.

The two friends shook their heads again.

"The beans are actually the seeds of a tree called the Theobroma cacao, which grows in tropical regions of the world. Theobroma means 'food of the gods' in Latin," said Rita.

"Wow, I didn't know that!" smiled the little mouse.

"Once the seeds have been harvested they are then fermented, dried, and roasted. They are then husked, which is called winnowed, and this isolates something called the nibs. It's the nibs that are rich in cocoa solids and cocoa butter. We buy the roasted nibs which makes things easier," said Rita.

"Is that ready to eat?" asked Albert.

Rita smiled.

"Not quite. The nibs are then put through a machine that slowly grinds them with sugar between two granite wheels, and that turns the nibs turn into liquid cocoa. This is then heated and becomes liquid chocolate," she said.

Albert began to lick his lips at the thought of all that melted chocolate and looked longingly at the vats of chocolate which were on the other side of the glass wall. The smell was overwhelmingly tantalising.

"If you come with me I will show you the moulds we use to make chocolate eggs and the bars," said Rita.

The little mouse was mesmerised by the vats. He just knew he had to taste some of the melted chocolate so, as Big Tony went off with the lady, Albert hid behind a table leg and waited.

Eventually, a man in a white coat came out of the glass room where the vats were and Albert saw his chance. The little mouse darted across the floor and through the door before it closed.

"I made it!" he said to himself as he gazed up at the large tanks.

Slowly he climbed up one of the legs that supported the vat of chocolate and finally reached the top and looked over the edge of the vat.

As the little mouse looked down into the large bowl full of chocolate deliciousness, his foot slipped and, before he knew it, he'd fallen into the vat.

Chapter 23

In a millisecond, Albert was covered from nose to tail in chocolate.

"Help! Help!" shouted the little mouse as he was knocked around by the large machine.

Rita heard the screams and rushed over to the machine. She quickly pressed the red stop button.

"Albert, are you ok?!" she asked.

"I think so, I slipped," replied Albert.

Rita gently lifted Albert out of the vat of chocolate and sat him down on the worktop.

"How did you get in here!?" she asked.

"Erm, the door was open," said Albert, feeling terribly embarrassed.

"Really? It shouldn't have been. Anyway, stay there while I fetch a cloth," she said and dashed off.

As Albert sat there licking chocolate off his hands, the chocolate in his fur started to set. All of a sudden, before he could do anything, the little mouse was unable to move.

"You look like a little chocolate mouse," laughed Big Tony. "Maybe we could put you on the shelf and see if someone buys you!"

Rita soon returned with a bowl of warm soapy water.

"Don't you worry, Albert, we will have you all cleaned up in no time," she said, placing the little mouse in the bowl.

Slowly the chocolate started to melt and after a few minutes, Albert was able to move again.

The little mouse took off his clothes and then started to clean the chocolate from his fur.

"Do you want me to try and clean your clothes?" Rita asked.

"No, thank you, don't worry. I have a spare set in my rucksack," said the little mouse.

Suddenly someone else came into the room to see what all the activity was about.

"What's happened?" they asked.

"Oh, hello Chris. It's fine, Albert just fell into one of the vats of chocolate, but it's all sorted now," said Rita.

When Albert was clean, he climbed out of the water and dried himself on the towel Chris had brought for him.

"This is the second time you've had to be rescued today," laughed Big Tony.

"It's not funny," said Albert. "I could have been eaten, again."

"Again?" asked the gull looking at his friend.

"Oh, didn't I tell you? A crab grabbed my tail when I was swimming this morning and was going to eat me," said Albert.

"Really?"

"Yes, really, and that was before I got caught in the riptide," muttered the little mouse.

"I never did like crabs," said Big Tony pulling a face.

Albert quickly got dressed.

Chapter 24

Albert felt embarrassed about the trouble he had caused and knew it was his fault.

"I'm so sorry for making a mess of your chocolate," he said.

"It's fine. We're just glad you are alright," said Rita as she put Albert's chocolatey clothes into a bag and placed them in his rucksack.

"I've survived worse," smiled Albert.

"Yes, and that was just today," chuckled Big Tony.

"Well, let me at least give you each a free chocolate egg?" she said.

"Certainly not," said Albert.

"Really, it's the least we can do, especially with the state your clothes are in," insisted Rita.

Albert agreed to accept the two chocolate eggs and then said goodbye to everyone at Salcombe Dairy Chocolate Factory.

Once the two friends were outside, Big Tony began to walk back down the road towards the quayside.

"Hey, where are you going?" shouted Albert.

"Albert, maybe we should go home before anything else happens to you?" said Big Tony.

"I doubt if anything else can happen. And, anyway, we haven't been to Salcombe

Dairy for ice cream," said the little mouse smiling.

"Ice cream?" asked the gull licking his beak.

"It's the best ice cream in the world, so they tell me," said Albert.

"Ok, but as long as you promise not to need rescuing again!" said Big Tony, chuckling.

The friends then walked in the direction of Island Street, past all the boat builders until they reached Salcombe Dairy.

Chapter 25

The little mouse and his friend sat down on the tall chairs and looked at all the different flavours of ice cream that were on display.

"I've never seen so many types," said Big Tony.

"Me neither," said Albert.

"Hello, I'm Ellen," said the lady behind the counter. "What can I get you?

"To be honest, there are too many to choose from. I thought there was only vanilla," said Albert. "Which one do you recommend?"

"We are famous for our honeycomb ice cream," said the lady, pointing to one of the tubs of ice cream in the cabinet.

"Honeycomb it is then, please!" announced Albert.

"Two, please!" said Big Tony.

"Are you here on holiday?" asked Ellen as she scooped the Honeycomb ice cream into two cones.

"Not exactly," said Big Tony. "We live in Dartmouth and are just here for the day, aren't we, Albert?"

"That's right. We came here by sea in my boat," said Albert.

Ellen stopped scooping and looked at the little mouse.

"I hope you don't mind me asking but are you Albert Mouse?" she asked.

"I am, and this is my friend Big Tony. Have you heard of us?" he asked, sounding surprised.

"My mother lives in Dartmouth and she met you when you were the Mayor. I think you visited her at home one day."

"Quite possibly. I did visit a lot of people at their homes on Victoria Road," said the little mouse.

"Now, tell me what you think of this," said Ellen as she passed the cones over the counter to the two friends.

Albert took a small bite of the ice cream.

"Oh, boy, that is scrumptious!" he said, licking his lips.

"Yes, I agree. That's the best ice cream I have had in my whole life and I've had a few, I can tell you," said the gull.

"I now know why it's your best seller," said Albert.

"Would you like a tour to see how we make our ice cream?" asked Ellen.

Albert looked at Big Tony, then looked at the lady.

"I'd like to but, to be honest, I'm not having a very good day today," said the little mouse.

"Oh no, what's happened?!"

"Well, first I nearly got eaten by a large crab and then I was washed out to sea by a rip tide and had to be rescued by the lifeboat. Then I fell into a vat full of chocolate and had to have a bath," said Albert.

"Gosh, you have had a bad day, but, listen, it's perfectly safe, trust me."

"If you're sure?" said Albert, finishing his ice cream and getting up.

The two friends went around the counter and followed Ellen into the Dairy.

Chapter 26

Neil, Tom and Ryan in the factory showed them how the ice cream was made. It was all very interesting. Albert made sure he stayed well back from the large vats of milk and cream just in case the worst should happen again.

At the end of the tour, Albert turned and looked at Big Tony.

"See, nothing happened!" he said smugly. "I'm still clean and didn't fall into anything."

The gull shook his head despairingly.

As Albert walked back to the counter he saw a mother and her daughter waiting to be served.

Suddenly the little girl saw Albert.

"Mouse!" she said, pointing at Albert.

She then screamed. Not just a short, little scream, but a high-pitched scream that went on for several moments.

Poor Albert was taken by surprise and was so scared that he darted for cover. In the process, he tripped and fell backwards into a tub of ice cream.

Ryan ran forward and gathered Albert out of the tub.

"Albert are you ok!?" he asked.

"I think so," said the little mouse, wiping the ice cream from his eyes so he could see.

Ryan looked at the child.

"It's ok, it's Albert Mouse," he said holding Albert up for the girl to see.

Albert held his hands over his ears in case the girl screamed again, but she didn't.

"Would you like to say hello to him?"

"Hello," said the little girl, who was still looking a little scared.

"Hello," said Albert. "What's your name?"

"Molly," said the girl.

"I'll sorry I scared you," said the little mouse.

"You did a little but now you're all covered in ice cream," said Molly.

The little mouse looked down at his shirt and trousers.

"It's ok, they needed a wash, anyway," said Albert, even though they were clean a few minutes earlier.

"We can sort that out for you, Albert, we have a washing machine at the back," said Tom.

A short while later, Albert's clothes had been washed, dried and ironed and there wasn't any trace of ice cream.

Albert and Big Tony said goodbye to Ellen, Neil, Tom and Ryan at Salcombe Dairy, and then to Molly and her mother.

"Here are some chocolate bars for the journey home," said Ryan, giving the two friends a bar each.

They said thank you and then walked down back onto Island Street.

"I think we had better go home before anything else happens," said Albert.

"Good idea," said Big Tony and they both walked back to the boat.

Chapter 27

Back at the pontoon, Big Tony untied the ropes while Albert took his sea chart and compass out of his rucksack.

"Are we all ready?" asked Albert, as Big Tony climbed aboard.

"Aye, aye, Captain!" said the gull and took up his usual position at the front of the boat where he could have a good view. "Make a heading for Dartmouth, Captain!"

The two friends slowly pulled away from the jetty and headed out of the estuary.

"Don't forget the Bar, Albert," said Big Tony.

Albert stuck his thumb up and turned the boat to starboard.

The little boat made its way out of the estuary and into the sea.

Albert looked up at the blue sky and smiled. He was glad to be heading home after his adventure in Salcombe.

As the little boat made its way along the coast back to Dartmouth Albert took the bar of chocolate out of his pocket and nibbled on it.

"I've had some narrow escapes today," he thought to himself. "But that's what happens when you are Dartmouth's greatest explorer."

It wasn't long before the little boat containing Albert and Big Tony passed Dartmouth Castle.

"Can you smell that?" asked Big Tony.

"Pasties?" replied Albert.

The gull shook his head.

"No, Albert, it's the smell of home," he said.

Albert smiled and headed for the quayside next to the Harbour Master's building.

Chapter 28

Albert tied the boat up and the two friends made their way to Higher Street.

As they pushed open the white wooden gate of No. 10, Millie leapt off the windowsill.

"Albert's home!" she shouted and rushed into the garden.

"You didn't die!" she said, hugging her brother.

"Of course I didn't!" said Albert smiling.

"He came close a few times," muttered Big Tony under his breath.

Just then Mrs Mouse appeared in the doorway and hugged her son.

"Oh, I've been so worried about you," she said.

"Why? We were fine, weren't we, Big Tony?" replied Albert.

"Absolutely," smiled the gull.

"Come on in and sit yourselves down. You must both be exhausted," she said taking Albert's rucksack from him.

Big Tony and Albert went into the house and sat down in the lounge, while Mrs Mouse went to make them a nice hot chocolate.

"Albert, did you eat your sandwiches?" asked his mother from the kitchen.

"Oh, sorry, I forgot about them," replied the little mouse.

"So, are you telling me that you've gone all day without any food?" asked his mother.

"No, we had a pastie and a sausage roll for lunch and then some ice cream," said Albert.

"I'll have the sandwiches if no one else wants them?" said Big Tony, who was already quite hungry again.

Mrs Mouse brought a tray into the lounge, placed it on the table and gave everyone a cup of hot chocolate.

"So, tell me all about your trip. Did you make it to Salcombe or have you been hiding near the castle all day?" asked his mother.

"Mum, of course, we got to Salcombe! It was just like Dartmouth, really," said

Albert sipping his hot chocolate. "Mum, did you know that this hot chocolate is made from the seeds of a tree called the Theobroma cacao? Theobroma means 'food of the gods' in Latin."

"Is it really?" asked Dorothy.

"Yes, we learnt that on our travels today, didn't we, Big Tony?" said Albert.

"We certainly did," said the gull.

"Oh, that reminds me. I've got some presents in here for you," said the little mouse and he took the bags of sweets out of his rucksack.

"There's one for you Mum and these two are for Millie and Dorothy," he said.

"These sweets are so tasty," said Dorothy as she chewed on one of them.

"They're from a shop called Cranch's. It's the oldest sweet shop in Devon," said Albert.

"I hope you were both well-behaved and didn't get into any trouble," said Mrs Mouse looking at Albert.

"Mum, we didn't get into any trouble and we always said please and thank you when we went into the shops," said the little mouse.

Chapter 29

For the rest of the evening, Albert and Big Tony told everyone about their adventures in Salcombe. Big Tony talked about meeting his relatives and how tasty the pastie and ice cream were.

Albert told everyone about the enormous crab that wanted to eat him and about meeting Alice and her dog called Spaghetti. He even told them about meeting Molly and the Mayor of Salcombe.

However, Albert didn't mention the fact that he'd had to be rescued by the RNLI and got to travel in two lifeboats. Neither did he mention falling into a vat of chocolate and a tub of ice cream.

When it was time for Big Tony to go home Albert walked his friend to the door.

"Erm, Albert, don't you think you should tell your mother about being washed out to sea?" whispered the gull.

"My Mum will only worry and if I tell her she might not let us go on another adventure," said the little mouse.

Big Tony looked at his friend and raised his eyebrows.

"And, anyway, it's not as if Mum will hear about it all the way over here in Dartmouth," said Albert

"Well, it's up to you I suppose. Just think about it and remember what happened last time when you didn't tell her you'd bought a boat?" said the gull

"Ok, I'll think about it," said Albert.

"Good," said Big Tony. "And thanks for an amazing adventure today!"

"You're welcome," smiled the little mouse.

As Albert closed the door his mother came out of the lounge holding a bag.

"Albert, what's this?" she asked.

"Oh, erm, yes, I had a bit of an accident with some chocolate."

"What kind of accident?" asked his mother.

"The weather was very hot in Salcombe and the chocolate bar that was in my pocket melted all over my clothes," said the little mouse.

"But it's over everything!" said Mrs Mouse.

"Like I say, it was very hot in Salcombe, it was almost tropical really, not at all like here," said Albert.

"Well, it was lucky you packed a spare set of clothes then wasn't it!?" asked his mother, as she took the bag of chocolate-covered clothes into the kitchen.

"That's exactly what I thought!" said Albert.

Chapter 30

Albert didn't take Big Tony's advice and soon forgot to tell his mother about the lifeboat, the chocolate or the ice cream.

However, a few days later his mother was sitting in her favourite chair reading the newspaper.

"Oh, you have to be kidding me!" she suddenly said.

"What is it?" asked Millie.

"It's Albert!" said Mrs Mouse.

Dorothy looked up from her colouring book.

Mrs Mouse cleared her throat and began to read the newspaper aloud.

"A major sea rescue occurred in Salcombe this week after it was reported that someone had been washed out to sea while swimming off North Sands. When the lifeboat crew arrived on the scene they were surprised to see that the swimmer was local Dartmouth celebrity Albert Mouse," read Mrs Mouse.

She paused slightly.

"On the way back to Salcombe the lifeboat suffered engine trouble after becoming caught in a fishing net. This meant that a second lifeboat had to be called to take Albert Mouse to medical attention. After a thorough medical assessment, Albert was allowed to continue his holiday in the South Hams town of Salcombe."

Mrs Mouse put the newspaper down.

"Albert Mouse, come down here this instant," she shouted.

"Albert's in trouble," sang Dorothy.

A few moments later, Albert popped his head around the door of the lounge.

"You called?" he said.

"Yes, I did and I'm not very happy," said his mother.

"Why, what's happened?" her son asked.

His mother opened the newspaper and read the article to her son. When she'd finished she looked at Albert.

"To be fair, Mum, it wasn't as serious as the newspaper is making out," said Albert.

"Go to your room and we will talk about this later," said his mother.

The little mouse slowly went back to his bedroom and lay down on his bed.

"I should have listened to Big Tony," he said to himself, staring at the ceiling. "I'll never be allowed to go on another adventure for as long as I live now."

To all the pupils at
Salcombe Primary School.
Thank you for writing such a
great adventure for me.
I think all your illustrations
are brilliant.
Well done everyone!
Best wishes.

Albert

The Albert Mouse Trail

Now you can visit the places that appear in the Albert Mouse books.

Just look for these blue stickers around Dartmouth and Salcombe.

Acknowledgements

By Appointment to
children's imagination

I'm grateful to Brian and Pam, the human owners of Cherub Cottage, for sharing their house with Albert and his family.

This story has been made possible by the pupils and staff of Salcombe Church of England Primary School. I'd like to thank them for creating such an amazing adventure for Albert. It's been an absolute joy to have been given a privileged glimpse into the children's minds as they imagined what Albert could get up to.

I'd like to thank Salcombe Dairy and Salcombe Dairy Chocolate Factory, The Bake House and Cranch's Sweet Shop for agreeing to be part of this story.

As always I am grateful to "Walter" for sending me the breeze that moves the willows.

About James Hywel

James Hywel is a children's author and creator
of both Mr Milliner and Albert Mouse.
He is a member of *The Royal Society of Literature,
The Society of Authors, The Writers Guild of Great
Britain* and *The Dartmouth & Kingswear Society*.

For more books and updates visit our website:
www.jameshywel.com

Remember to sign up for our blog
https://jameshywel.com/blog

Albert met with Sarah from Break the Cycle and decided he needed his own company name. He remembered receiving a letter that said *To Albert Mouse Esq.*
"Yes," he thought. "That's me!"

Albert Mouse Esq. helps children and young people benefit from bespoke educational programmes that support their development, helping them to navigate their thoughts and feelings, and appreciate their time in and out of school. Thus, supporting positive relationships and challenging negative behaviour.
Albert is excited to be visiting schools with his friend Sarah to talk to children who are feeling anxious, nervous, upset, worried or confused. Albert feels many of the same feelings as other children his age do.

www.jameshywel.com/break-the-cycle

Part of Break The Cycle C.I.C.

Company Number 14265959

Printed in Great Britain
by Amazon